Heart of a Fighter

Sue Leather & Julian Thomlinson

Series Editor: Rob Waring
Story Editor: Julian Thomlinson
Series Development Editor: Sue Leather

HEINLE
CENGAGE Learning™

Australia • Brazil • Japan • Korea • Mexico • Singapore • Spain • United Kingdom • United States

HEINLE
CENGAGE Learning™

Page Turners Reading Library

Heart of a Fighter
Sue Leather & Julian Thomlinson

Publisher: Andrew Robinson

Executive Editor: Sean Bermingham

Senior Development Editor:
Derek Mackrell

Assistant Editor: Sarah Tan

Director of Global Marketing:
Ian Martin

Content Project Manager:
Tan Jin Hock

Print Buyer:
Susan Spencer

Layout Design and Illustrations:
Redbean Design Pte Ltd

Cover Illustration: Eric Foenander

Photo Credits:
43 Scott Feldstein/Flickr,
44 Francis Specker/Landov

ISBN-13: 978-1-4240-4643-0

ISBN-10: 1-4240-4643-2

Heinle
20 Channel Center Street
Boston, Massachusetts 02210
USA

Cengage Learning is a leading provider of customized learning solutions with office locations around the globe, including Singapore, the United Kingdom, Australia, Mexico, Brazil, and Japan. Locate your local office at:
international.cengage.com/region

Cengage Learning products are represented in Canada by Nelson Education, Ltd.

Visit Heinle online at **elt.heinle.com**

Visit our corporate website at
www.cengage.com

Printed in the United States of America
2 3 4 5 6 7 – 14 13 12 11

Contents

Background Reading

People in the story

Dwayne Williams
Dwayne is the captain of Brenton College's taekwondo team.

Minho Kim
He is a student at Brenton College. He comes from Korea. He is a very good taekwondo fighter.

Professor Melanie Saunders
Professor Saunders is coach of the taekwondo team at Brenton College. She helps students with their problems.

Randy Gordon
Randy is Dwayne's roommate.

Jack Garcia
Jack is a friend of Dwayne and is on the college taekwondo team.

Clark
Clark is the security guard at Brenton College. He was a very good boxer a long time ago.

This story is set in Brenton, a college town in the northwestern United States.

Chapter 1

The new king

"Hi, everyone." Dwayne Williams smiled as he walked into the college taekwondo training hall for the first time since the break for vacation. Nine or ten students were already warming up in the training hall, or *dojang*. They said "hi" to the captain of the Brenton College taekwondo team as he walked in.

Dwayne looked at himself in the long mirror that went all along one side of the *dojang*. He looked good, he thought. His white suit, or *dobok*, was still clean and it looked nice. He did a few practice kicks in front of the mirror. *Yes*, he thought, *looking good*. Dwayne was the taekwondo team's best fighter, and he knew it.

"How's it going?" asked Jack Garcia. Jack was on the team, too. The tall young man hit Dwayne on the back.

"Good," said Dwayne. He smiled. "Vacation in Hawaii was great . . ."

Suddenly, Dwayne stopped talking. He nodded his head toward the corner of the training hall.

"Who's that?" he asked, looking toward a young Asian man with a black belt. The man was warming up with great concentration.

"He says his name is Kim," said Jack. "Everyone just calls him Kim, he says. I never saw him before. Just come from Korea, he says."

"Korea, eh?" Dwayne looked at the new student. Now he was practicing his basic kicks. *He looks good,* Dwayne thought, but he said, "Well, we'll soon see what 'Mr. Korean Black Belt' can do."

"Yeah," Jack smiled.

Kim turned and saw Dwayne and Jack watching him. He gave them a big, friendly smile. Dwayne nodded back at him.

Just then, Professor Melanie Saunders, the coach of the Brenton College taekwondo team and fifth *dan* (rank) black belt, walked in. There were now over twenty students in the *dojang*. When they saw Coach Saunders, they quickly got into lines by the color of their belts. In a few seconds, they were in order, from the white belts to the higher black belts. The students didn't move as the coach looked at them. She was looking to see if they were clean and neat. Coach Saunders was very tough, but she was a good coach, and the students had a lot of respect for her.

"Welcome back," Saunders finally said in her surprisingly loud voice. "And welcome to our new students. Especially Mr. Kim, who joins the college from Korea. I'm sure you will all learn a lot from him."

Kim smiled. But Dwayne looked to the front, his face not showing any feeling. *Huh,* he thought. *What are we going to learn from him?*

Saunders led the twenty-five students in the traditional bows to herself and to the *dojang*. Then the training started. The class started with basics. Basic skills were, as Melanie Saunders liked to say, "the beginning and end of taekwondo." For an hour, the students moved up and down in their lines, as Saunders taught them. They all worked hard at their basic standing positions, or stances, their punches and their kicks.

But Saunders was never happy. "Come on, black belts," she shouted. "You're not working hard enough!"

Dwayne's face was wet with sweat. He was feeling very, very tired. The truth was that he didn't train at all on vacation, and he ate too much. Next to him, Jack was also sweating. Dwayne looked around at the others. Kim was having no trouble at all. He didn't even look tired.

"Sparring!" called Saunders.

Toward the end of every class, the students sparred. Sparring was free fighting in pairs. It was a time for the students to practice by fighting their partner and to get ready for competition.

Sparring was Dwayne's favorite part of the class. He was a good fighter, he knew. That's why he was the team captain. He walked toward Kim. *This is my chance to show this guy a thing or two*, he thought.

Kim bowed to Dwayne, still smiling, and the two men started sparring. Dwayne was the bigger and taller of the two. He tried to catch the Korean with one of his kicks, but Kim was fast and Dwayne couldn't hit him. Dwayne looked into Kim's eyes and saw that he was very determined, but very calm.

Saunders watched as the two black belts fought hard. Dwayne tried hard to hit Kim, but he was getting tired. Kim looked just the same, still with his big smile. That smile! What was he so happy about? Dwayne asked himself. It made him angry. *I'll give you something to smile about*, he thought. But Kim was too fast.

Finally, Dwayne was really tired and he found it difficult to move. Now Kim went forward, kicking and punching hard. Dwayne got hit in the body by a very powerful kick from the young Korean fighter.

Now everyone in the class was watching the fight between the two black belts.

"Wow! This new guy's really good!" Jack said to the other black belts.

"Yeah," said one of the others. "He's really beating Dwayne! Look at him!"

Everyone looked at Dwayne. His legs were heavy and he wasn't moving much. "Stop!" called Saunders.

9

Kim bowed to Dwayne. "Thanks," he said, smiling. "I learned a lot from that."

After class, Dwayne left the *dojang* quickly. As he turned to bow to the training hall, he saw that all the students were standing around Kim. He was still smiling.

Chapter 2

Help from above

Dwayne went straight to his room at Robert Adam House. He didn't want to see anyone in the locker room, where everyone changed after the class. He had bruises all over his body from the fight with Kim, and he was still angry. Dwayne hoped that Randy, his roommate, was still at football practice.

But Randy was in their room. "What happened to you?" he asked as Dwayne walked into the room. "Did a bus hit you?"

"Ha ha ha," said Dwayne. He took a bag of ice from the ice box and put it on the bruise over his eye, then said, "That's not funny."

"Did someone give you that at practice?" asked Randy. He gave Dwayne a juice and they sat down on their beds, looking at each other.

The two friends drank the juice for a few moments, not speaking. Then, Dwayne told his friend about Kim and the fight.

". . . he really beat me," Dwayne finished. He looked down.

"Come on!" said Randy. "It's just one of those things.

You know you're the best. You'll get him next time."

"I guess," said Dwayne.

"I'm going out for a run. Want to come?" asked Randy. Randy was on the college football team. He ran every day to keep fit.

"No, thanks," said Dwayne. "Another time, maybe."

Randy went out and Dwayne lay on his bed, thinking. He thought about the fight with Kim again. He knew it wasn't "just one of those things" as Randy said. This Kim was good. Really good.

◇◇◇

The next day, Dwayne didn't go to his taekwondo class at four o'clock. He lay on his bed in his room while the two-hour class went on. At 6:15, Dwayne's cell phone rang. He looked at the number. It was Coach Saunders. He didn't answer it.

At around 6:30, Dwayne left his phone on his bed, got up, and went out to the store to buy some juice. He was walking back into Robert Adam House when he heard someone calling him from above.

"Hey, Dwayne!"

Dwayne looked up. It was Clark. He was the security guard, which meant that he looked after the building and knew all the students.

"Hey," said Dwayne.

"I heard you got beat," said Clark.

"What?"

"Some new guy," said Clark. "I heard he really beat you!"

"I'm coming up," said Dwayne.

Dwayne went upstairs to Clark's door. He really liked to talk to the old guy. He had an interesting past. He was a really good boxer in his time, fought in the war, and worked in business. He knew a lot about the world.

"So what happened?" asked Clark as they went into his sitting room.

Dwayne looked at the older man. Clark was short and well built. He really looked like a boxer. Dwayne sat down in a comfortable armchair, and Clark gave him a cold drink. Dwayne told Clark about the fight. The security guard listened carefully as Dwayne talked.

". . . so I guess he was just better than me," Dwayne finished.

"It happens," said Clark. "It happened to me when I was boxing. But remember, losing doesn't make you a loser. If you lose and you don't learn anything, then, well, *then* you're a loser."

Dwayne didn't speak for a while.

"You know, he said that, at the end. Kim. He said, 'I learned a lot from that.' I guess he learned how to beat me black and blue."

Clark laughed.

"Listen, Dwayne, I'm serious. What did *you* learn?" Clark asked.

"I don't know. You know, the worst thing was," Dwayne went on, "he was smiling all the time."

"Smiling, huh? And you got angry about that, did you?"

Dwayne nodded his head, thinking to himself.

"He sounds smart, this new guy. He sounds like a guy you can learn a thing or two from," Clark said, getting up. "Well, you'd better go on and get studying."

Dwayne stood up, too. "Thanks, Clark," he said.

"That's OK, Dwayne. And remember. If you *don't* learn something, next time he'll beat you black and blue again!"

Chapter 3

Watching and learning

Dwayne thought about it late into the night. The next day, he went to his taekwondo class feeling much calmer. *Getting angry was the problem,* Dwayne told himself. *Today, when Kim smiles, I'll smile right back at him.* He arrived half an hour early for the four o'clock class to warm up. Kim was already there.

"Hi," said Kim, smiling at Dwayne.

"Hi," said Dwayne, smiling back.

"I enjoyed our sparring together," Kim said.

I'm sure you did, thought Dwayne, but he kept on smiling.

Dwayne moved to the other end of the *dojang* to get ready. *Watch and learn,* he told himself. He watched Kim as he got ready for the class. He looked at the way that he kicked and punched. Were his techniques really that good? Or did he have something else?

"Where were you yesterday, Dwayne?" asked Coach Saunders.

"Sorry, Coach," said Dwayne. "My stomach. Something I ate, I think." He looked away, but he knew that Saunders saw everything.

Saunders looked at Dwayne carefully. "Mmm . . ." she said. "Well, I want to see you train hard today."

The class started. Dwayne concentrated and worked hard. He watched Kim as much as he could.

After basics, it was time for more sparring. Coach Saunders put the students into pairs.

"OK," said Saunders. "You two, together." She went around all the class, putting the students into pairs. "And you two," she said, finally, looking at Dwayne and Kim.

Dwayne faced Kim and smiled. Kim sent a big, friendly smile right back at him. They bowed and started practicing. Kim moved forward and kicked out his front leg. Dwayne was too slow. The kick hit his chest, hard, and he fell down to his knees.

There was a pain in Dwayne's chest, and he couldn't stand up at first. Kim held out his hand to Dwayne to pull him to his feet, but Dwayne didn't take it. He got to his feet slowly.

"Hey, are you OK?" Kim asked. "Do you want to rest?"

"I'm fine!" Dwayne said.

Stay calm, Dwayne told himself. They started again, and this time Dwayne tried to kick and punch Kim. But Kim was too fast, and Dwayne couldn't hit him. He felt himself getting tired. Then Kim attacked, and soon Dwayne was on the floor again.

Stay calm, he told himself. *You must stay calm.*

Dwayne stayed calm. But Kim still beat him again, and again.

◇◇◇

"Look at it this way—now you have nothing to worry about," said Clark. Dwayne and Clark sat in the security office later that evening. The Seahawks were playing the Forty-Niners on the small TV in the corner.

"What do you mean, I have nothing to worry about?"

"You lost, is what I mean. You don't have to worry who's the best now. He's the number one now. He's got all the worries. It's a lot easier for you than for him."

Dwayne looked at Clark.

"Think about it," Clark explained. "He won. So he's worried. Will he win again?"

Dwayne still looked unhappy.

"Yeah, but . . ."

"But what?"

"But I want to be number one. I want to be the best."

"Are you sure about that?"

"What do you mean?"

"Dwayne, I've been watching you for the last two years. I know you miss training. I know you party when you need to rest. When you train, you sometimes take it easy. You want to be the best? Then you've got to start *doing* your best."

Dwayne didn't say anything. He was angry, but he knew Clark was right.

"Listen," said Clark. "I was the same as you. I won all the time; I thought I could never lose. Then in 1966 I lost the College Championships to Brad Kane. I mean, I really lost. He beat me easily. It was the worst moment of my boxing life."

"Really?"

"I was surprised. Shocked," Clark went on. "But after the shock, I thought 'I have to change something.' I accepted that Kane beat me because he was fitter than me. Better in every way. So I learned something and after that I changed. I changed what I ate and what I drank. I changed my training, everything. You understand? I worked a lot harder and I got really fit. Next year, I was a better fighter. I won the Championships."

"But . . ."

"Next year, I beat that Brad Kane," Clark went on. "I beat him easily. I learned something and I made a good change."

Clark moved his head closer to Dwayne's and looked into the young man's eyes. His face was serious. "Now, are you going to learn? Are you going to learn it now, or when it's too late?" he asked.

Dwayne didn't reply.

"What you have right here, Dwayne, is a change moment. Now, is it going to be a bad change or a good change?"

Chapter 4

Black belt

Later that night, Dwayne lay in bed and thought. He thought about Clark's words. *Good change or bad change.* He thought about Kim. The Korean was fit, really fit. Dwayne wasn't that fit. Clark was right—he didn't train hard enough. He knew that. He liked to eat a lot, and he didn't exercise enough. Maybe if he got fitter . . .

Next day, Dwayne asked Randy, "Can I run with you?"

"Sure," said Randy.

Dwayne changed into his running shoes and ran with Randy around the college campus. It was hard. His friend was very fit. Footballers have to be fit because they have to run a lot. Dwayne found it hard to run as fast as him. But after the run, he felt good.

"I'll run with you when I can," Dwayne said to Randy.

From then on, Dwayne ran almost every day, sometimes with Randy, sometimes on his own. He started training harder, too. Little by little, he felt fitter. He found that he could train longer and felt his taekwondo slowly get better. One morning, he saw Kim running toward the park and decided to run after him.

"Mind if I run with you?" Dwayne asked.

"Hey, sure, Dwayne," Kim said, smiling.

They ran round the park without talking. At the end of it, both were tired.

"Thanks for that," said Kim. "I enjoyed it." He began to leave.

"So how do you like Brenton?" Dwayne asked.

"It's great. I'm very happy to study here."

"How about our little *dojang* here? Is it very different from back home?"

Kim laughed.

"It's *very* different."

"Different how?" Dwayne asked.

Kim thought about it, then said, "How long did it take you to get a black belt, Dwayne?"

"I was sixteen when I started, so . . . about two, three years, I guess."

"I started taekwondo when I was four years old," Kim said. "I trained almost every day of my life. On my eighteenth birthday, my father gave me my black belt. It took me fourteen years, training every day. That is what I mean by *different*."

◇◇◇

About a month later, Coach Saunders said, "OK, listen, everyone. Here's the timetable for the training camp." In two weeks the students had a training camp at a beautiful place near the Cascade Mountains. The training camp happened every year, and everyone enjoyed it. It was something different from the normal training in the *dojang*. It was hard work, but it was fun, too.

Good, thought Dwayne to himself, *I can train really hard at camp.* He was running with Randy every day now, and he was beginning to feel a lot fitter. His taekwondo was better too, he thought.

Coach Saunders told the students to get into pairs for practice. Dwayne walked up to Kim. As always, Kim was smiling. *OK*, thought Dwayne. *Let's see if you're still smiling at the end of this.* It was time to see if he really was better.

Kim came forward, kicking and punching. Dwayne blocked him, then kicked and punched back. The two of them were much closer than before. One minute went by, then two, then three. Dwayne was breathing hard, but so was Kim. And Kim was no longer smiling. *I must be doing something right*, thought Dwayne.

Kim kicked at Dwayne's legs, but Dwayne jumped high and kicked out at Kim's chest. Kim didn't block quickly enough, and the kick put him on the floor. Kim got up, but he was different. Now he was angry. He ran forward, kicking and punching. They both fell down, but continued fighting on the floor.

"Look at those two!" The students all stopped their practice and watched Kim and Dwayne as they fought.

"Stop this now!"

The two men didn't hear Coach Saunders. They went on fighting.

"Stop!!!" Coach Saunders shouted louder. Dwayne and Kim heard her this time.

"Get out of the *dojang*, both of you. Now!" she shouted.

Dwayne and Kim stopped fighting immediately and walked out of the *dojang*.

As she left, Saunders looked at the other students. "Get back to your practice," she said.

◇◇◇

"I'm surprised at both of you," said Saunders.

"Sorry, Coach," said Kim and Dwayne.

"It wasn't Dwayne, Coach. It was me," began Kim.

"Mr. Kim, I know it is different from Korea here because I have trained there. But here, in my *dojang*, you will follow my rules. Do you understand?"

"Yes, Coach."

"Now please leave. I want to speak to my team captain."

"Yes, Coach," he replied, and walked off to get changed.

"What was that, Dwayne?" Saunders went on. "That was a very bad example for the other students. You're a black belt and the team captain!"

"I'm sorry, Coach. But about being the captain. I want to speak to you about that."

"Oh? And what do you want to say about it?" asked Saunders.

"Well, I think Kim would be a better captain this year. He's better than me. He started this when he was four years old."

"I see. You want to be the coach instead?"

"I don't understand, Coach."

"Well, Dwayne, the coach decides the captain, as I remember. You want to decide the captain? That means you want to be the coach, doesn't it?"

"I didn't mean . . ." Dwayne began.

"Let me worry about choosing the captain. You worry about training hard and not having stupid fights, please."

"Coach," said Dwayne, "I'm really, really sorry. It won't happen again." Dwayne looked the coach in the eyes. He looked serious.

"Well, good," she replied. "Because if it happens again . . ."

"It won't happen," said Dwayne.

Coach Saunders smiled as she watched Dwayne leave the *dojang*. Dwayne was changing, she thought. He was finally becoming a man. Maybe he was even becoming a true student of taekwondo.

Chapter 5

Training camp

The week of the training camp arrived. The coach and students went by bus to the camp. The camp was in a beautiful part of the Washington State countryside, with the Cascade Mountains high above them. There were forests and waterfalls near the camp, and the air was clean and fresh. The training at camp was different from training back at college, too. Coach Saunders tried to do something different every day. There were a lot of fitness exercises outside, as well as the usual basics and sparring.

The first two days, Dwayne tried to keep away from Kim. Dwayne wanted to show the coach that he was serious when he said "never again." But it was impossible to keep away completely. The two of them didn't talk much, but when the coach asked the students to run, Dwayne looked over at Kim to see if he was faster. When they sparred, each one tried to be the best. One time it was Kim who won. The next time it was Dwayne.

On day three of the training camp, Saunders took them climbing in the mountains. The students had to climb in pairs. "You two," she said to Dwayne and Kim, "together." Dwayne looked at his coach. Did she really want them to have to climb together? But as he looked at her face he knew she was serious.

"Come on," said Dwayne to Kim. "We have to work together." The two students put on their climbing boots and got everything ready for the climb. They needed rope, some food, and water. It was a long, hard climb to the top of the mountain, and they had to get ready carefully.

When the climb started, Dwayne said "I'll go first." Kim just smiled. Dwayne climbed up the rock ten meters and then stopped. "Come on," he called to Kim. Dwayne held the rope as Kim climbed up. A few moments went by as Kim climbed up the rock. Dwayne couldn't see Kim. Suddenly, Dwayne felt the rope go heavy. "Hey!" shouted Dwayne. "Are you all right?"

"I'm fine!" called Kim from below. But he wasn't fine, Dwayne could see. He was about to fall. Kim's foot slipped off the rock. His face was red.

Dwayne pulled the rope hard. "It's OK!" called Dwayne. "I've got you!"

For a minute or two, Dwayne held the rope tight, as Kim tried to find a place for his foot again. It felt like an hour. Sweat was falling from Dwayne's face. *Come on, Kim*, he thought. *Don't fall.* At last, Kim found the place with his foot and started climbing again carefully, slowly.

"Are you OK?" asked Dwayne.

"I told you, I'm fine," Kim replied.

They went on climbing. It was a hard climb and they didn't get to the top until two hours later. At the top of the mountain, they both stood and enjoyed the quiet and the clean air. They looked at the view all around them. They could see mountains and snow everywhere around them. It was beautiful!

"Look at that!" said Dwayne, smiling. It felt really wonderful, standing there in the snow. "Good job!" he said to Kim, smiling and putting his hand up. Kim looked him in the eye. "Good job," he said, hitting Dwayne's hand, but he didn't smile.

◇◇◇

The next day, the students practiced sparring again. Late in the class, Dwayne found Kim and sparred with him. Kim seemed tired, and Dwayne could see he was still upset about the climb, about needing help. Dwayne hit him a few times with kicks and punches. After he fell down, Kim punched the floor hard, then got up looking very serious. Quickly, he attacked Dwayne by taking his leg, holding him in the air, then throwing him hard to the ground.

Dwayne shouted in pain as he hit the floor. "Hey, what was that? That isn't taekwondo!"

"That's just your problem," said Kim, standing over him. "You're not a real fighter. You don't have the heart of a fighter. Real fighters don't worry about danger.

Real fighters don't worry about rules," said Kim. He turned away from Dwayne.

Kim turned around and began to walk away. Dwayne got up and held his arm.

"I'll show you a real fighter," Dwayne said, quietly. Kim smiled at him.

"How about a real fight, then?" asked Kim.

Dwayne looked at Kim. "OK!" he said.

"Outside the *dojang*?" Kim asked.

"Outside the *dojang*."

"Tomorrow, five o'clock in the morning. Near the trees just outside the camp."

"OK," said Dwayne. "I'll be there."

Chapter 6

The fight

At five o'clock the next morning, Dwayne and Kim met just outside the camp.

"Let's go," said Kim.

"Where?"

"I'll show you," replied Kim. "Come on."

The two men walked up through the forest. They didn't speak. It was a difficult walk and as they went up the air got colder. After about thirty minutes, Dwayne heard the noise of water. A lot of water. A few moments later, he saw a huge waterfall.

"OK," said Kim, looking at the waterfall. "We're here. Now we'll see who's a fighter and who isn't."

"What's this?" asked Dwayne.

"We stand under the waterfall and see who can stand there for the longest time," he said.

Dwayne knew that things like this were often part of training in the past. But he looked at the huge amount of water and he didn't like it. "I thought you said a fight," he said.

"This is a fight, all right," said Kim. "You'll see. Or if it's too cold for you, we can go back to camp?"

Was the Korean serious? Dwayne looked at Kim's face and he could see that he really was serious. "Well, if you can do it," he said, "I can do it, too."

"Let's go, then," said Kim.

The two men walked into the waterfall. Dwayne was shocked when he felt the power of the water. He couldn't breathe at all, and it was difficult to stand. He looked at Kim, fighting the water next to him. *He's right*, thought Dwayne. *It really is a fight.*

"Had enough?" shouted the Korean.

Dwayne tried to shout back, but no words came out.

The Korean fighter was standing in a taekwondo stance, his face showing pain and concentration.

Dwayne did the same. Both of them were shaking with the cold. Dwayne stood in a taekwondo stance under the icy waterfall. Seconds, minutes went by. The water was very powerful and very cold but after a moment or two, Dwayne began to feel calm. He thought about Clark's words. A change moment, Clark said. *I'm changing,* Dwayne thought, and realized he wasn't shaking. Then, under the icy water, he finally understood. He understood that taekwondo was not about winning fights with Kim, or with anyone else. It was about winning the fight with himself. As he thought this, Dwayne felt very calm. He looked over at Kim. Kim was watching him.

He looks afraid. Maybe I need to help him, Dwayne thought. Then everything went black.

◇◇◇

"Dwayne! Come on, Dwayne!" Dwayne could hear a voice from far away. It was Kim. He tried to open his eyes, but couldn't. Then the voice became louder. At last, he opened his eyes and saw Kim's face. Kim looked very serious. He was pulling him up, helping him out of the very cold water.

"I'm sorry," said Kim. "I didn't want this to happen . . . I'm very sorry."

Dwayne found it hard to move alone. Kim got Dwayne out of the water, and somehow, onto his feet. It was difficult as he was shaking so much. Kim put Dwayne's arm around his own neck and started walking. "Come on, Dwayne," he said again. "Please be OK."

They walked very slowly back to the camp, falling down every few meters. Two kilometers from the camp, they fell down for the last time.

Chapter 7

Heart of a fighter

Dwayne opened his eyes and looked around him.

"Dwayne!"

"Coach Saunders."

Dwayne was in a hospital bed. Coach Saunders was next to him. She looked worried.

"What happened?"

"You almost died. That's what happened. I went to breakfast and found out from the other students that you and Kim were not in the camp," she said, "I guessed you were together, and I sent everyone to look for you."

"I don't know what to say," said Dwayne.

"Jack and two other students found you," the coach went on. "You were very lucky. It was just in time." Dwayne thought about the icy water.

"Where is Kim?"

"In the next room," said the coach. "He's resting. And you have to rest, too."

Dwayne got out of bed. He still didn't feel good, but he almost ran to the next room and opened the door. Kim was lying in bed. His eyes were closed and he looked bad. *Do I look this bad?* Dwayne asked himself. He guessed he did.

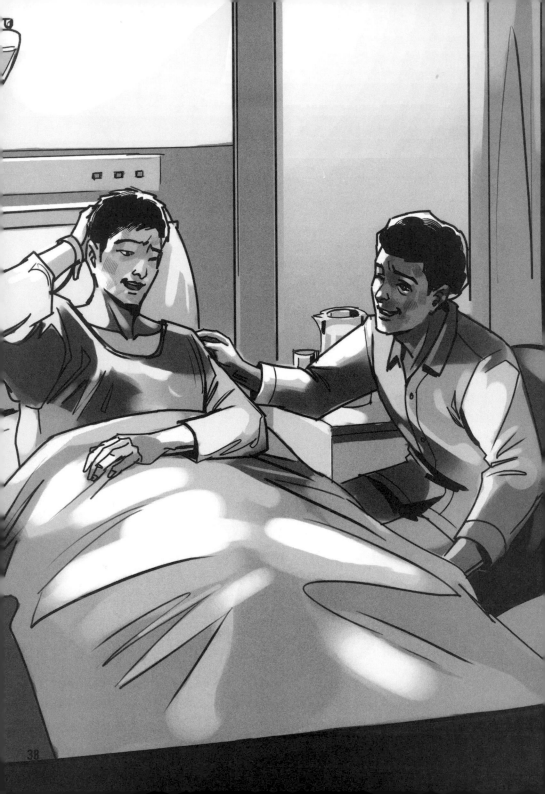

"Get back to your bed, Mr. Williams," said the doctor who was standing next to Kim's bed.

"Can't I talk to him?"

"It's all right," said Kim, opening his eyes.

"Five minutes, then back to bed," said the doctor, as she left.

Dwayne moved painfully to the chair by Kim's bed and sat down. At the same time, Kim pulled himself up in the bed so he was sitting.

"You all right?" Kim asked.

"Yeah, I'm OK," said Dwayne. "You?"

"I'm good. I'm good."

They sat for a few minutes without speaking.

"I want to say thank you . . ." Dwayne began.

"You don't have to," Kim said. "It was my idea. It was a stupid thing to do."

"I thought you did this training in Korea," Dwayne said.

"We do. But not on our own. Someone always pulls you out, so you don't stay in the water too long. It's too dangerous."

"I see," Dwayne said.

Again, they sat for a while without speaking. Then Kim spoke.

"I want to tell you something," he said. "I didn't like you, Dwayne. All my life, I've been the best, the top student. I told you, I've trained all my life. And you've trained three, four years, and you start to beat me."

"But . . ." Dwayne started.

"No, please listen, I want to say this," Kim said. "It's very hard for me. When I first saw you, I could see you were very strong. I was afraid of you. Even when I beat you, I was afraid. That's why I said those things. That's why I said that you weren't a real fighter, that you didn't have the heart. Because I was afraid, and angry with myself for losing. I'm so stupid."

Dwayne looked at Kim sitting in his bed. After today, he thought there was nothing more to learn, but he saw now he was wrong. This young man, from the other side of the world, was just the same as him. Just like him! He thought about all their fighting and started to laugh.

"Hey, it's not funny," said Kim.

"I know. I know . . ." started Dwayne, but he was laughing too much.

Kim watched him for a moment, then smiled. Soon he was laughing, too. They sat in the hospital room and laughed so hard it was painful.

Review

A. Match the characters in the story to their descriptions.

1. _____ Dwayne Williams
2. _____ Jack Garcia
3. _____ Melanie Saunders
4. _____ Minho Kim
5. _____ Randy Gordon
6. _____ Clark

a. Dwayne's friend and teammate
b. Dwayne's roommate and a football player
c. the coach of the Brenton taekwondo team
d. the captain of the Brenton taekwondo team
e. a security guard at Brenton College
f. a taekwondo fighter new to Brenton College

B. Complete each sentence with the correct word from the box.

dojang	sparring	belts	captain
dobok	stance	bow	

1. In taekwondo, the way you stand when fighting is called your _____.

2. When fighters practice free fighting in pairs, it is called _____.

3. The place people practice taekwondo is called the _____.

4. Before each fight, taekwondo fighters _____ to each other.

5. The white clothing a taekwondo fighter wears is called a _____.

6. The leader of the taekwondo team is called the _____.

7. Taekwondo fighters wear _____ of different colors to show their level.

C. Choose the best answer for each question.

1. Why does Dwayne feel tired during his first taekwondo training?

  a. He is not feeling well.

  b. He trained too much over the holidays.

  c. He did not train at all over the holidays.

2. Why doesn't Dwayne go for his second taekwondo training?

  a. He is feeling tired from the day before.

  b. He does not want to lose to Kim again.

  c. He is too busy talking to Clark.

3. What lesson does Dwayne learn from Clark?

  a. He has to train hard if he wants to be the best.

  b. He has to learn some new taekwondo moves.

  c. He has to control his temper.

4. According to Kim, how is taekwondo is different in Korea compared to the U.S.?

  a. People start doing taekwondo from a young age.

  b. It is much easier to get a black belt in Korea.

  c. There are much better taekwondo fighters in Korea.

5. What does Dwayne discover about Kim and himself in the end?

  a. They were both afraid of each other at first.

  b. They both want to be number one.

  c. They both do not like Professor Saunders.

Background Reading:
Spotlight on . . . *Taekwondo*

Taekwondo is a popular Korean martial art and the national sport of South Korea. The word taekwondo comes from the Korean language and means "the way of kicking and punching."

There are two main forms of taekwondo. The traditional form originates from ancient Korea and is mainly for self-defense. The modern way, which is practiced at the Olympics and other events, focuses more on speed and competition. Both forms are based on kicks or punches from a standing position.

There are many levels of taekwondo. The junior section has ten levels, or ranks, with each level having a different color—usually starting with a white belt and finishing with a red belt with a black stripe. The senior ranks are called dan, all of which have a black belt but with various ranks (first dan, second dan, and so on). To move from one level to the next, students have to complete promotion tests in front of teachers or judges. It can take many years of practice to get a black belt.

Amazing martial arts feats!

- B.J. Penn, pictured on the left, is a famous mixed martial arts fighter who can jump out of an empty swimming pool from a standing jump without using his hands.

- Anthony Kelly from Australia can catch flying arrows with his hands.

- Masutatsu Oyama, a Japanese citizen born in Korea, fought and defeated almost 270 people in his life. He could also kill bulls with his bare hands.

- Chad Netherland can break 50 blocks of ice in less than 20 seconds. He also held two planes from taking off for over a minute.

- A 72-year-old Chinese woman pulled a four ton (3,600 kg) truck for 10 meters using only her teeth. She has been training her teeth with 30 years of martial arts.

- Taekwondo instructor Mustafa Dasan from Jordan used his elbow to break 5,000 kg of marble and cement bricks in one minute and sixteen seconds. In the same event, Mustafa also let another man use a jackhammer (a tool used to drill holes in cement) on his stomach.

Think About It

1. Have you tried a martial art? Which one?

2. Why do you think martial arts such as taekwondo, are so popular?

Glossary

beat	(v.)	If you beat someone, they lose and you win.
block	(v.)	If you block a person's punch, it does not hit you.
bow	(v.)	When you bow to someone, you stand in front of them and move your upper body and head down to show respect.
boxer	(n.)	someone who fights in a ring.
bruise	(n.)	a black-and-blue mark on your body from an injury
captain	(n.)	the leader of a sports team
concentrate (-ation)	(v.)	If you concentrate on something, you are thinking very hard about it.
fit	(adj.)	If you are fit, your body is in very good condition for sports.
pair	(n.)	two of something
pass out	(v.)	If you pass out, you feel weak, fall to the ground, and lose consciousness.
punch	(v.)	to hit someone with your closed hand
respect	(v.)	to think highly of someone
rope	(n.)	a long piece of material people use to climb mountains
security guard	(n.)	a person who looks after a place to protect it
shock	(n.)	a great surprise
spar	(v.)	In taekwondo, if you spar with someone, you practice fighting with them.

stance	(*n.*)	the way that you stand
sweat	(*n.*)	the water that comes from your skin when you are hot
technique	(*n.*)	a method or way to do something
waterfall	(*n.*)	where a lot of water comes off a high place